AMERICAN MUSEUM ᴼꜰ NATURAL HISTORY

INSIDE STARS

by Andra Serlin Abramson
and Mordecai-Mark Mac Low

STERLING CHILDREN'S BOOKS
New York

STERLING CHILDREN'S BOOKS
New York

An Imprint of Sterling Publishing
387 Park Avenue South
New York, NY 10016

Library of Congress Cataloging-in-Publication Data Available
Lot#:
10 9 8 7 6 5 4 3 2 1
07/11

Published by Sterling Publishing Co., Inc.
387 Park Avenue South, New York, NY 10016

www.sterlingpublishing.com/kids

© 2011 by Sterling Publishing Co., Inc., and American Museum of Natural History
Distributed in Canada by Sterling Publishing
c/o Canadian Manda Group, 165 Dufferin Street
Toronto, Ontario, Canada M6K 3H6
Distributed in the United Kingdom by GMC Distribution Services
Castle Place, 166 High Street, Lewes, East Sussex, England BN7 1XU
Distributed in Australia by Capricorn Link (Australia) Pty. Ltd.
P.O. Box 704, Windsor, NSW 2756, Australia

Printed in China
All rights reserved

Sterling ISBN: 978-1-4027-7709-7 (hardcover)
978-1-4027-8162-9 (flexibound)

For information about custom editions, special sales, premium and corporate purchases, please contact Sterling Special Sales Department at 800-805-5489 or specialsales@sterlingpublishing.com.

Design by Celia Fuller

Previous page: Thousands of young stars in a nearby galaxy—called the Large Magellanic Cloud—are shown in a photo taken by the Hubble Space Telescope.

This page: Bright stars illuminate the clouds of gas and dust from which they recently formed in the Carina Nebula, approximately 7,500 light-years from Earth.

Cover image: Newly born stars are emerging from the cloud of gas and dust in which they formed. This is the region NGC 602 in the nearby galaxy known as the Small Magellanic Cloud.

How to Read This Book

This book is different from most you've read. Many of its pages fold out—or flip up! To know where to read next, follow arrows like these ➡ and look for page numbers to help you find your place. To access more information about stars, download Microsoft's free Tag Reader on your smartphone at **www.gettag.mobi**. Look for tags that look like this ▦ throughout the book. Use your smartphone to take a picture of the tag, which will link to related information, pictures, and videos at the American Museum of Natural History's website. If you don't have a smartphone, use the URLs listed on page 47. Happy exploring!

Image Credits: NASA, ESA and the Hubble Heritage Team STScI/AURA)-ESA/Hubble Collaboration (cover); NASA, ESA (page 1); NASA, ESA and Jesús Maíz Apellániz (Instituto de Astrofísica de Andalucía, Spain) (pages 2–3); shutterstock.com, © John Wollwerth (pages 4/9); Precision Graphics (page 5); Lunar and Planetary Institute (page 6); Photo Researchers, Inc., © Eckhard Slawik (page 7); NASA Marshall Space Flight Center (NASA-MSFC) (page 8); shutterstock.com, © Yuriy Kulyk (pages 10–11, background); Precision Graphis (pages 10 & 11); ESO/H.H.Heyer (page 12); Corbis, © Roger Ressmeyer (page 13); Corbis, © Ed Darack/Science Faction (page 14, top); NASA, 2002 (page 14, bottom); Precision Graphics (page 15); Photo Researchers, Inc., © Mark Garlick (pages 16/21); NASA, ESA, R. Windhorst (Arizona State University) and H. Yan (Spitzer Science Center, Caltech) (pages 17–20, bottom); © American Museum of Natural History (page 17); NASA/JPL-Caltech/K. Gordon (Univ. of Ariz.) & GALEX Science (pages 18–19, top); NASA, ESA, M.J. Jee and H. Ford (Johns Hopkins University) (page 20, top); Precision Graphics (page 22); Robert Gendler/NASA (page 23); NASA, ESA, and the Hubble Heritage Team (STScI/AURA) (page 24); NASA/ESA/M. Livio and the Hubble 20th Anniversary Team (STScI)(page 25); Harvey Richer (University of British Columbia, Vancouver, Canada) and NASA (page 26); NASA (page 27); NASA (page 28); Precision Graphics (page 29); X-ray: NASA/CXC/SAO/F.Seward; Optical: NASA/ESA/ASU/J.Hester & A.Loll; Infrared: NASA/JPL-Caltech/Univ. Minn./R.Gehrz (page 30); NASA and G. Bacon (STScI) (page 31); SDO/AIA (pages 32/37); Precision Graphics (page 34); ESA/Science Source/Photo Researchers, Inc. (page 35, top); SOHO (ESA & NASA) (page 35, bottom); Photo Researchers, Inc., © Atlas Photo Bank (page 36, left); SOHO (ESA & NASA) (page 36, right); Precision Graphics (page 37, top); © American Museum of Natural History (page 38); © American Museum of Natural History (page 39, top); SOHO (ESA & NASA) (page 39, middle); © American Museum of Natural History (page 39, bottom); NASA, ESA and Jesús Maíz Apellániz (Instituto de astrofísica de Andalucía, Spain) (pages 40–41); NASA/CXC/M.Weiss (page 41, top); Getty Images, © Stuart O'Sullivan (page 42); NASA/ESA/A. Fujii (page 45).

CONTENTS

What's Out There?

With so many different objects out in space, how can you tell what you are seeing? A telescope makes it easier for you to get a good look at faraway things. But even without a telescope, you can probably figure out what you are seeing in the sky. If a bright light is moving or blinking, it's most likely an airplane or satellite. Planets, like Venus, Mars, or Jupiter, look like steady pinpoints in the sky. Stars, on the other hand, seem to twinkle and flicker.

Our Sun and all the astronomical objects bound to it by gravity are called the solar system. This illustration shows the relative sizes of the orbits around the Sun of six planets.

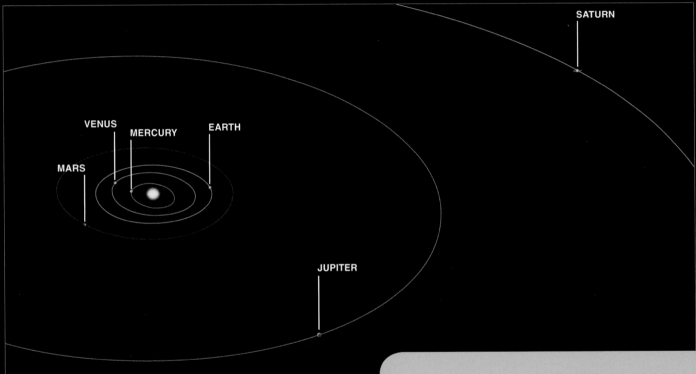

SPACE FACTS

Our home, the Earth, is a planet. It orbits the Sun, which is a star. Seven other planets also orbit our Sun (Mercury, Venus, Mars, Jupiter, Saturn, Uranus, and Neptune), along with at least three dwarf planets (Ceres, Pluto, and Eris), and thousands of asteroids. Hundreds of planets have been discovered orbiting stars other than our Sun.

Word Power

STARS: balls of hot gas that shine from their own energy.

PLANETS: round objects in space that orbit, or travel, around a star, shine from reflected starlight, and are much larger than anything else in their orbit.

MOONS: natural objects in space that orbit planets and shine by reflected light.

Planets

Moon

Stars

Satellites

Meteors

Horizon

Airplanes

5

THE NIGHT SKY

On the next clear night, when it gets dark, take a look
up in the sky. There are a lot of things up there. You
might see airplanes, satellites, and planets. But mostly
what you'll see are stars. People have been wondering
about stars for thousands of years. Today, we know a
lot about them. Join us as we go inside the stars and
discover what makes them important to us.

The Constellations

Long ago, people looked up into the sky and noticed patterns in the stars. These patterns are called constellations. People in many cultures have made up stories to go along with the constellations and have given them names. To the ancient Greeks, for example, some patterns looked like animals, such as the constellation known as Taurus the Bull. Others looked like people, such as Orion the Hunter.

During the summer months in the Northern Hemisphere, if you look up, you might see the Summer Triangle in the southern sky, connecting the brightest stars in the constellations Lyra the Lyre, Cygnus the Swan, and Aquila the Eagle.

Deneb

Vega

CYGNUS

LYRA

Summer

AQUILA

Altair

POSITION OF THE STARS

Thousands of years ago, astronomers noticed that the position of the lights in the sky seemed to change as the seasons changed. Back then, people believed that the Sun and other stars revolved around the Earth. Today, we know that the Earth actually revolves around the Sun.

As the Earth moves around the Sun, different constellations can be seen in the night sky at different times of the year. This is because the part of the sky that we see at night changes as the Earth's position in relation to the Sun changes.

THE IMPORTANCE OF STARS

The next time you step outside on a sunny day, feel the heat of the Sun, our closest star, on your face. Think about how important that heat is to us here on Earth. Without that heat, our planet would be frozen solid. The Earth is at a distance from the Sun that allows it to support life. If Earth were much farther away from the Sun, the planet would be too cold. If it were much closer, it would be too hot.

The distance from the Earth to the Sun is about 93 million miles (150 million kilometers).

If you think of the Earth rotating as a spinning top, the Earth's axis is actually tipped slightly to one side. As the Earth travels around the Sun, its tilt does not change. The place on Earth where the Sun shines the longest each day changes from above to below the equator. This change gives us the hot and cold seasons we experience each year.

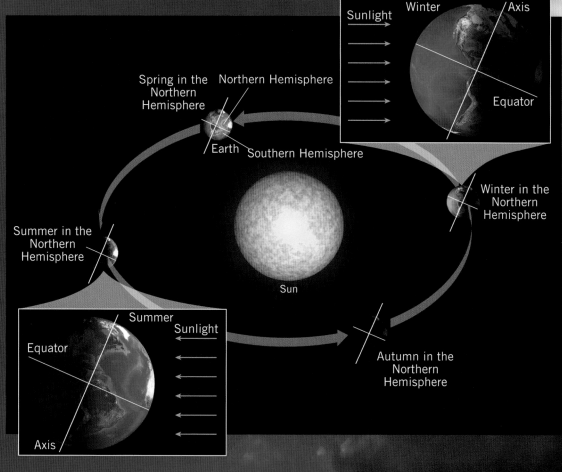

Sunlight Winter Axis
Equator

Spring in the Northern Hemisphere
Northern Hemisphere
Earth Southern Hemisphere

Summer in the Northern Hemisphere

Winter in the Northern Hemisphere

Sun

Autumn in the Northern Hemisphere

Summer
Sunlight
Equator
Axis

Only five to ten of the brightest stars can usually be seen from big cities, while thousands of stars can be seen when looking up at a dark sky in the country.

There are thousands of satellites orbiting the Earth.

Satellites like this one are common in Earth's orbit. Without them, global positioning systems, cell phones, satellite TV, and other devices would not work; weather forecasts would be far less reliable; and our knowledge of the Earth and stars would be far more limited.

Types of Telescopes

Scientists use a variety of telescopes to study the stars. Different types of telescopes are used by astronomers to view all wavelengths of light emitted from stars, from radio to visible to X-ray. The mirrors of the largest optical telescopes, which can see the faintest objects, now exceed 30 feet (10 meters) in diameter, while the antenna of the largest radio telescope is more than half a mile (1 kilometer) across. Several telescopes can even be linked together over great distances (thousands of miles, in the case of radio telescopes) to observe in extremely fine detail.

HOW SCIENTISTS STUDY THE STARS

Since the Sun is too bright to look at directly, and other stars are so dim that only their positions and colors can be measured with the naked eye, scientists have had to find other ways to study the stars. The invention of the telescope about 400 years ago was a big step forward for astronomers. It allowed them to discover stars and planets never seen before. Ever since then, people have been improving on the design. The very first astronomical telescopes magnified an image only eight times more than what you can see with your eyes, much like a pair of modern binoculars. Today, telescopes can grasp light from stars billions of light-years away, giving astronomers incredible new information about the Universe.

Astronomers work together with the four (27-foot) 8.2-meter mirrors of the Very Large Telescope in Chile.

SPACE FACTS

The first astronomical measurements were maps of the sky made before the invention of the telescope. These revealed that, from our perspective on Earth, other planets in our solar system appear to move past the stars. Careful measurement of these motions led sixteenth-century astronomer Nicolaus Copernicus to propose that the Earth and other planets travel around the Sun.

The Sun and Weather

The Sun causes sunny days, of course, but it also causes rainy, snowy, and windy days, too. This is because the Earth's hydrologic system, powered by the Sun, is responsible for all these types of weather. Thanks to the Sun's ability to change water from a liquid to a vapor, the water on Earth is constantly being recycled, and the weather systems carry the water from oceans to land.

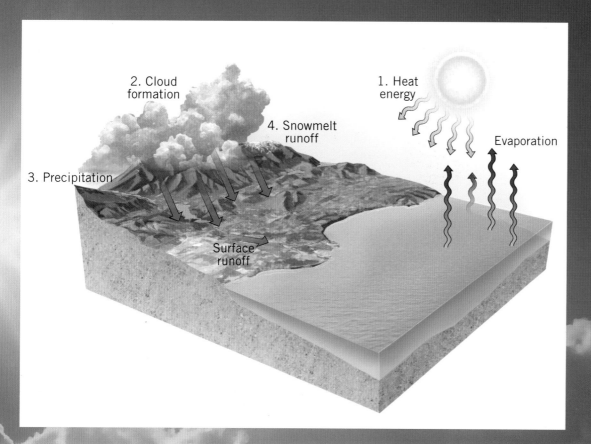

2. Cloud formation

4. Snowmelt runoff

1. Heat energy

Evaporation

3. Precipitation

Surface runoff

1. The Sun heats the oceans, causing water to evaporate into the air.

2. Water vapor condenses from the warm air as it rises, forming clouds made up of water droplets. As clouds form, the condensation of the water heats the air, raising its pressure. Winds blow from regions of higher pressure to regions of lower pressure, carrying clouds along.

3. When the clouds can't hold the moisture any longer, they release it in the form of rain or snow (precipitation), depending on the temperature.

4. This process is also the source of all of our fresh water, including snowmelt runoff from mountains and rain (surface runoff).

Word Power

CONDENSATION:
the change from a vapor or gas to a liquid.

EVAPORATION:
the change from a liquid to a vapor or gas.

THE BUILDING BLOCKS OF LIFE

The Sun is our closest star. But it isn't the only one that's important to us. Earlier generations of stars—going back to the very first ones—produced all the elements in the periodic table other than hydrogen and helium. When those stars died, they released these elements into space, where they became the building blocks of other stars, planets, and even life. These elements include the calcium in your bones, the iron in your blood, and the oxygen that you breathe.

Use your smartphone to scan here and learn more about the importance of stars.

The enormous 33-foot (10-meter) mirror of the Keck telescope in Hawaii allows observation of stars and galaxies that are billions of light-years away.

Space Travel and the Stars

• •

Earth is so far away from the next closest star beyond the Sun that people can't travel there even in the fastest spacecraft ever built. The Sun is almost 93 million miles (150 million kilometers) from the Earth. The next nearest star is more than 400 thousand times as far away and would take more than 200 thousand years to reach at the speeds traveled by today's spacecraft. Even traveling at the speed of light, the journey would take more than four years.

In fact, the size of the Universe is so great that it's hard to even imagine. To make it easier, we can think of enormous things as being tiny. Then we use that scale to make comparisons to even larger things, keeping the same proportion of measurements. For example, if we said that the Earth's orbit around the Sun, which has a radius of 150 million kilometers, had a radius of only 1 centimeter, then the nearest star would be over 400 thousand centimeters (4 kilometers) away, the galaxy would be 100 thousand kilometers across, and the Observable Universe still immense on this scale at 13 billion kilometers!

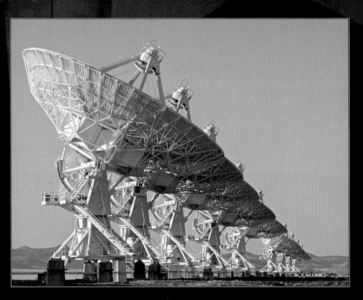

Radio telescopes such as the Very Large Array in New Mexico make images of distant stars and galaxies emitting radio waves just like optical telescopes make images of distant objects emitting visible light.

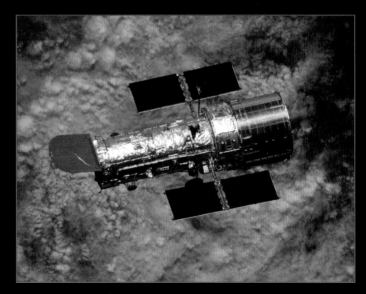

The Earth's atmosphere blurs images and absorbs infrared, ultraviolet, and X-ray light. So, to observe wavelengths of light that cannot reach the ground, telescopes such as the Hubble Space Telescope have been launched into orbit—some around the Earth and others around the Sun.

THE BIG BANG

Have you ever wondered how space and time began? It may be difficult to imagine, but evidence shows that some 13.7 billion years ago the entire Universe was very, very tiny—smaller than an atom. The Universe was extremely hot and dense, and began to quickly expand in all directions. It has been cooling and expanding ever since. We call this the "Big Bang." At first, the Universe was uniform, but gravity eventually caused galaxies, stars, and planets to form.

THE OBSERVABLE UNIVERSE

While no one knows whether the Universe goes on forever, we do have a limit to how much of it we can see. The vast region from which light has had time to reach us since the Big Bang is called the Observable Universe.

The Observable Universe has been expanding ever since the Big Bang occurred 13.7 billion years ago.

300,000 yrs

The First Stars

Immediately after the Big Bang, there were no stars at all. While astronomers don't know for sure when the first stars came into existence, their calculations show that they formed around 300 million years after the Big Bang.

These very first stars were made of hydrogen and helium gas. They were probably huge, perhaps more than 100 times the mass of our Sun. These enormous stars lived for "only" a few million years before dying in spectacular explosions called supernovas. These supernova explosions produced the first elements in the Universe that were heavier than hydrogen and helium. It may sound incredible, but your body actually contains about a teaspoon's worth of the material that was formed more than 13 billion years ago by those very first stars.

SPACE EXPLOSION

A supernova is an explosion that shines as brightly as an entire galaxy for a few days. It occurs when a massive star uses up its fuel, and its outer layers can no longer resist the force of its own gravity. Supernova explosions form many of the elements on the periodic table.

The very first stars were massive balls of hydrogen and helium gas. A computer simulation of the formation of one of these stars is shown here. These stars didn't last long. They burned up their fuel and exploded in gigantic explosions called supernovas.

Scientists hope to find the first galaxies that formed after the Big Bang by using the James Webb Space Telescope, scheduled for launch after 2014.

This million-second-long exposure with the Hubble Space Telescope reveals galaxies of all ages, back to shortly after the first stars formed.

Galaxies

Most stars are found in galaxies. Galaxies are large groups of millions to trillions of stars, along with gas and huge amounts of dark matter—all held together by gravity. There are more than 100 billion galaxies in the Observable Universe. The galaxy we live in is called the Milky Way.

Rainbow Colors

A prism spreads light into a rainbow or spectrum so all the individual colors can be seen. Different types of atoms and molecules emit and absorb very specific colors, so astronomers can study the spectrum of light emitted by a star to learn what elements make up that star.

Light moves at a speed of 186 thousand miles (300 thousand kilometers) per second. This is called the speed of light.

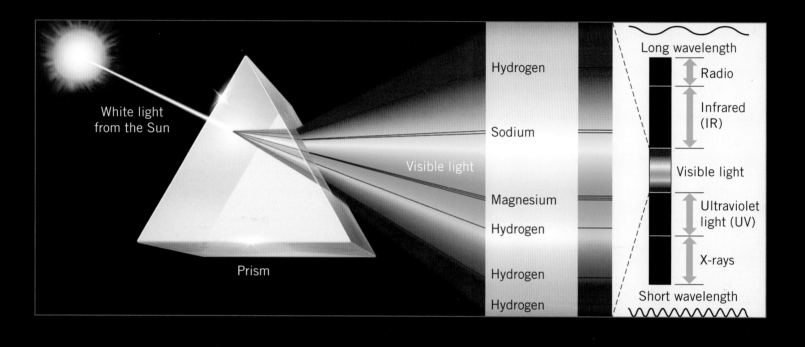

White light from the Sun

Prism

Visible light

Hydrogen
Sodium
Magnesium
Hydrogen
Hydrogen
Hydrogen

Long wavelength
Radio
Infrared (IR)
Visible light
Ultraviolet light (UV)
X-rays
Short wavelength

HOW LONG IS A LIGHT-YEAR?

A light-year is the distance that light travels in one year, which is 6 trillion miles (10 trillion kilometers). We can also use light-minutes (11 million miles or 18 million kilometers), and light-hours (700 million miles or a billion kilometers) to measure distance. Light-minutes and light-hours are sometimes used to measure distances within our solar system. The Sun is eight light-minutes away, while Neptune is four light-hours from Earth. Light-years are needed to measure the large distances between stars. The closest star to the Sun, Proxima Centauri, is just a little more than four light-years away.

LIGHT FROM THE PAST

When astronomers study stars, they are looking at light from the past. This is because stars in the most distant galaxies are so far away that it takes the light that they give off millions or even billions of years to reach us here on Earth. So the light that we see when we observe distant galaxies through a telescope is actually from a long time ago. The stars that emitted that light may have already exploded or evolved in some other way.

HOW STARS FORM

If you look up at the Milky Way on a dark night, you can see dark patches. These are clouds of space dust silhouetted against the stars of the galaxy. Space dust is made up of extremely fine grains of elements like silicon and iron. These clouds are where stars are formed. Star formation begins when a region in one of these clouds gets so dense that it begins to collapse in on itself. Gravity then draws even more gas in. This greatly increases the pressure, density, and temperature of the cloud. Finally, the pressure gets so high in the cloud's core, or center, that atomic nuclei are fused, or joined, together to form larger atoms. This process releases enormous amounts of energy and prevents further collapse. When these nuclear fusion reactions start, a star is born.

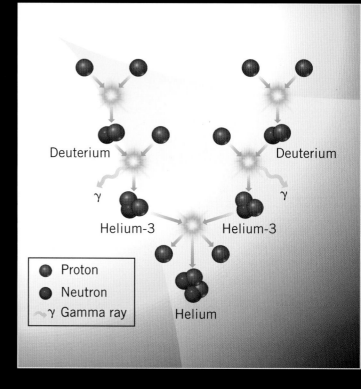

Deuterium   Deuterium

γ   γ

Helium-3   Helium-3

- ● Proton
- ● Neutron
- γ Gamma ray   Helium

In stars like our Sun, hydrogen nuclei (protons) fuse together to make larger atomic nuclei. This nuclear fusion reaction begins when two protons combine to create deuterium or heavy hydrogen. Deuterium fuses with an additional proton to make helium-3 (helium with only one neutron). When helium-3 forms, a lot of energy is released in the form of gamma rays. This energy is what powers normal stars. The addition of one more proton makes normal helium (helium-4). Stars can emit energy until they exhaust the hydrogen fuel they were born with. Once this fuel runs out, the star begins to die.

Word Power

ATOMIC NUCLEUS: the tiny center of an atom made of protons and neutrons. The plural form of nucleus is nuclei.

NUCLEAR FUSION: when two atoms collide hard enough that their nuclei combine, or fuse, into one larger atomic nucleus. Many nuclear fusion reactions release large amounts of energy.

This image of the Andromeda galaxy is a combination of an infrared image taken by the Spitzer Space Telescope, and an ultraviolet image taken by the Galaxy Evolution Explorer. Young, hot, high-mass stars shining brightly in ultraviolet light are shown blue, while older stars brighter in the near ultraviolet are shown in green. Cool, dusty regions where stars are forming and low-mass stars are shown in red. The bright yellow spot at the galaxy's center shows a dense population of older stars.

Dark Matter

If you can't see, touch, or sense something, how do you know it's there? That's the case with dark matter, invisible mass that we have only detected because its gravity affects how other things around it move. Observations and experiments increasingly support the theory that dark matter is made up of a kind of elementary particle that's new to science, and that it makes up approximately 87 percent of the mass in the Universe.

The dark matter in this cluster of galaxies is shown in blue and can be detected by how its gravity bends the light of distant galaxies traveling past the cluster, distorting their shapes.

Use your smartphone to scan here and learn more about galaxies.

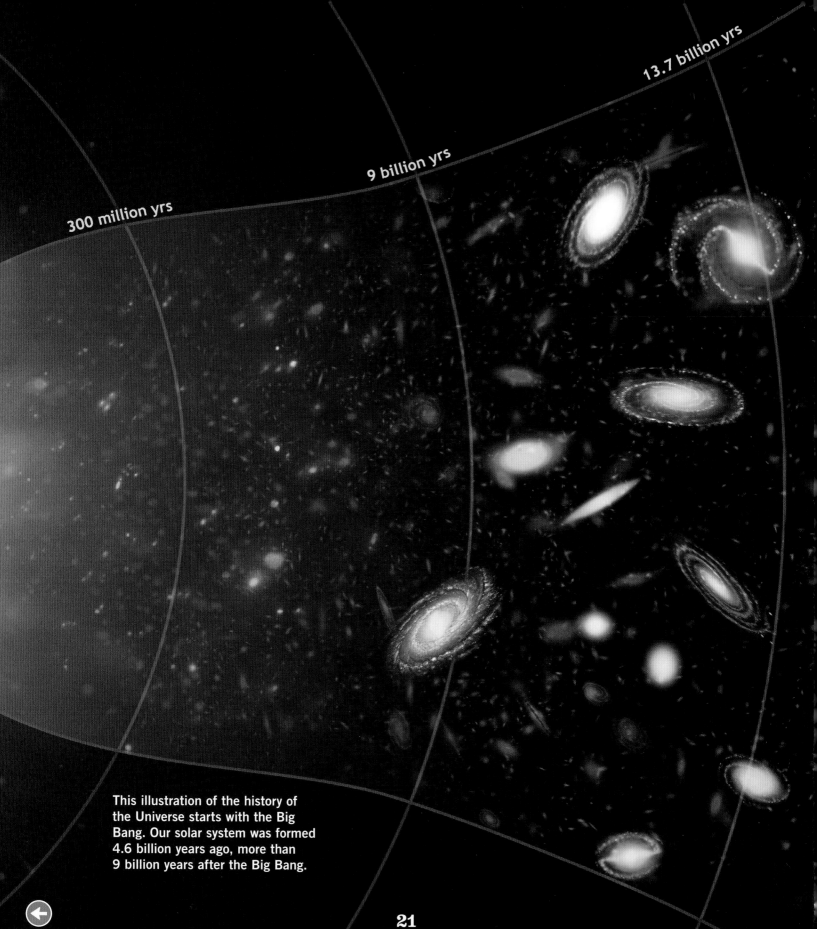

300 million yrs

9 billion yrs

13.7 billion yrs

This illustration of the history of the Universe starts with the Big Bang. Our solar system was formed 4.6 billion years ago, more than 9 billion years after the Big Bang.

Star Clusters: The Nurseries of Stars

Stars can form alone or in small groups, but most are born in huge stellar "nurseries" where thousands to millions of stars form together in one large gas cloud. Smaller groups of stars quickly move apart, but large groups tend to remain bound, by their own gravity, into star clusters. There are two main types of star clusters: *Open clusters* are more spread out, contain thousands to tens of thousands of stars, and exist for only small fractions of galaxy ages. *Globular clusters* are denser, can contain millions of stars, and exist for as long as galaxies.

A Young Cluster: Pleiades

Also known as the Seven Sisters, the Pleiades is one of the open star clusters closest to Earth. It can easily be seen in the night sky, in the constellation Taurus. The Pleiades is full of young, hot blue stars that shine much brighter than the Sun would at the same distance. Open clusters like the Pleiades don't hold on to their young stars for long. Over a period of a few hundred million years, their stars will get thrown out of the cluster until none are left.

STAR CRASHES

The stars in globular clusters are packed so closely together that they are always whirling around in the cluster. Near the center of these clusters, the stars are so crowded that they can slam into each other and form new stars. Nowhere else in the Universe are stars likely to run into each other.

A Globular Cluster

This image, which looks like a whirl of shiny flakes sparkling in a snow globe, shows many hundreds of thousands of stars moving about in the globular cluster called M13, which is 25,000 light-years from Earth. M13 is one of the brightest and best-known globular clusters in the northern sky. It is visible during the winter in the constellation Hercules.

SPACE FACTS

The difference between a tiny galaxy and a large globular cluster is that the mass of a galaxy is made up of mostly dark matter, while the mass of a globular cluster is made up of mostly stars.

The Carina Nebula

This photo, taken by the Hubble Space Telescope, shows the top of a three-light-year-long pillar of gas and dust in which gravity is pulling gas together to form new stars. The pillar is also being pushed apart from within, as infant stars buried inside it fire off jets of gas that can be seen streaming from towering peaks like arrows sailing through the air.

HOW STARS ARE CLASSIFIED

The next time you see stars up in the night sky, take a careful look. At first, they may all look the same. However, if you take the time to study them a little more, you can see that some are much brighter than others and some have noticeably different colors from others. Stars can appear to be brighter or fainter to us because of their varying distances, but even if we were able to view them all from the same distance, we'd see that they have very different levels of luminosity. Faint stars can be almost 100 thousand times less luminous than our Sun, while bright stars can be a million times brighter.

Word Power

LUMINOSITY: the brightness of a star compared to the brightness of our Sun, when viewed from the same distance. Stars that are more luminous can be seen from greater distances.

All these stars lie at just about the same distance from us, in the globular cluster M4. Yet, some appear far brighter than others because they have higher luminosities.

The Color of Stars

· ·

The color of a star depends on its temperature, which in turn depends on its mass and size. Cooler stars have a reddish tinge, like red-hot iron, while the hottest stars glow blue-white, like a lightning bolt. The hottest blue-white stars have surface temperatures of 18,000°F (10,000°C) and higher. The cooler yellow stars like our Sun are 10,000°F (5,500°C), and the coolest red stars are just a few thousand degrees.

Even massive blue-white stars turn red at the ends of their lives.

A colorful assortment of the hundreds of thousands of stars residing in the crowded core of a giant star cluster.

Star Mass

Our Sun has about twice the mass of the average star. The most massive stars have about 100 times the mass of the Sun, while the least massive stars have only about 8 percent of the mass of the Sun. Higher-mass stars are much rarer than lower-mass stars. This means there are far more low-mass stars than high-mass stars in the Universe. A star's mass determines how high the pressure and temperature are in its center. Higher temperatures mean much faster nuclear fusion, so more massive stars burn faster, hotter, and brighter.

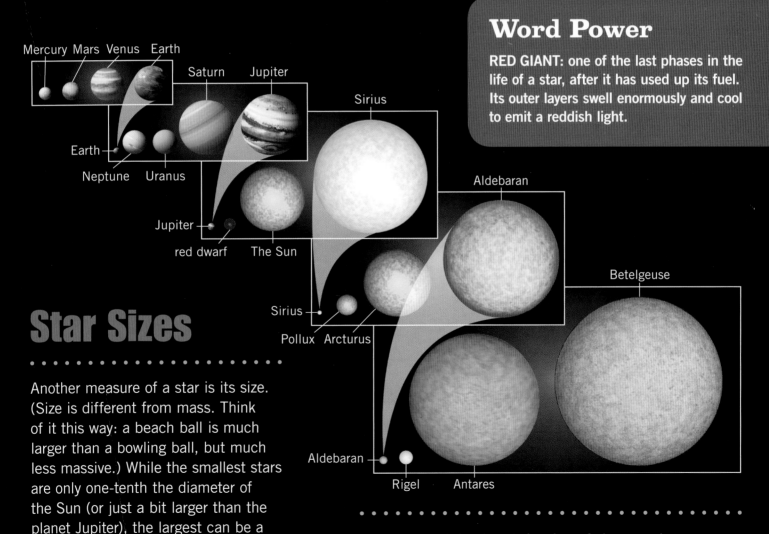

Star Sizes

Another measure of a star is its size. (Size is different from mass. Think of it this way: a beach ball is much larger than a bowling ball, but much less massive.) While the smallest stars are only one-tenth the diameter of the Sun (or just a bit larger than the planet Jupiter), the largest can be a thousand times the diameter of the Sun, or more. That's even larger than

This diagram shows the relative sizes of planets and stars. Jupiter, the largest planet in our solar system, is much smaller than our Sun, which in turn in much smaller than a large star

Star Age

The most massive stars run out of fuel for nuclear fusion after just a few million years. This is thousands of times faster than our Sun, which will have a life span of about 10 billion years. Scientists have calculated that some of the least massive stars will have lives as long as a trillion (1,000 billion) years.

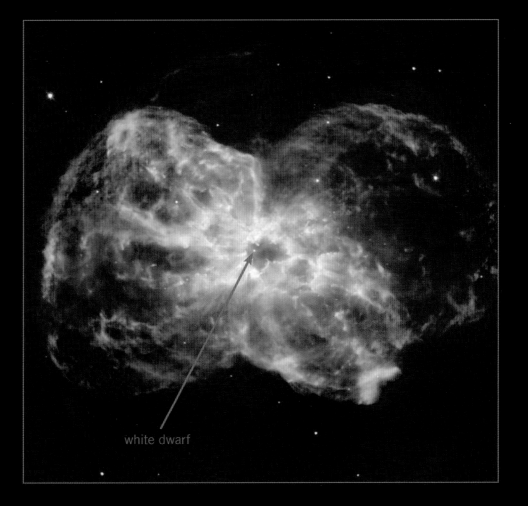

white dwarf

After stars run out of hydrogen fuel for nuclear fusion, they go through a time of burning elements such as helium and carbon, and then they shed their outer layers. Their cores then collapse to form black holes, neutron stars, or, for the vast majority of stars, white dwarfs. A white dwarf is shown here in the center of the layers of gas it has expelled.

DYING AND DEAD STARS

Like living things, stars have a life cycle. They are born, they mature, and eventually they die. Like a car running out of gas, stars die when they run out of fuel.

When fusion stops heating the gas in the center of a star, its own gravity causes the core of the star to shrink. As it is squeezed, it temporarily gets hotter. This causes the outer layers to puff out, forming an enormous red giant. The most massive stars then explode as supernovas, leaving behind black holes or neutron stars. Less massive stars like our Sun lose their outer layers more gradually.

Neutron Stars

Most stars turn into white dwarfs at the end of their lives. Their cores cool until the atoms are pressed up against each other, like a giant crystal the size of the Earth. In more massive stars (originally more than 8 times the mass of the Sun), the core of the star continues to collapse from the size of the Earth to the size of a city. It forms something like a giant

neutron star

The Crab Nebula is the remnants of a star that exploded as a supernova almost a thousand years ago, leaving behind a neutron star embedded in a

Black Holes

Black holes are formed by the most massive stars at the end of their lives. Inside these stars, gravity squeezes the core so that it becomes smaller and denser. The pull of gravity is so strong that nothing can get out, not even light, which is why it's called a black hole. Black holes do not look like big, black "holes" in space. In reality, they can only be detected by the effect they have on objects around them.

Word Power

BLACK HOLE: an object so dense that nothing can escape its gravity, not even light.

The sphere around a black hole, from which nothing can escape, not even light, is called an event horizon.

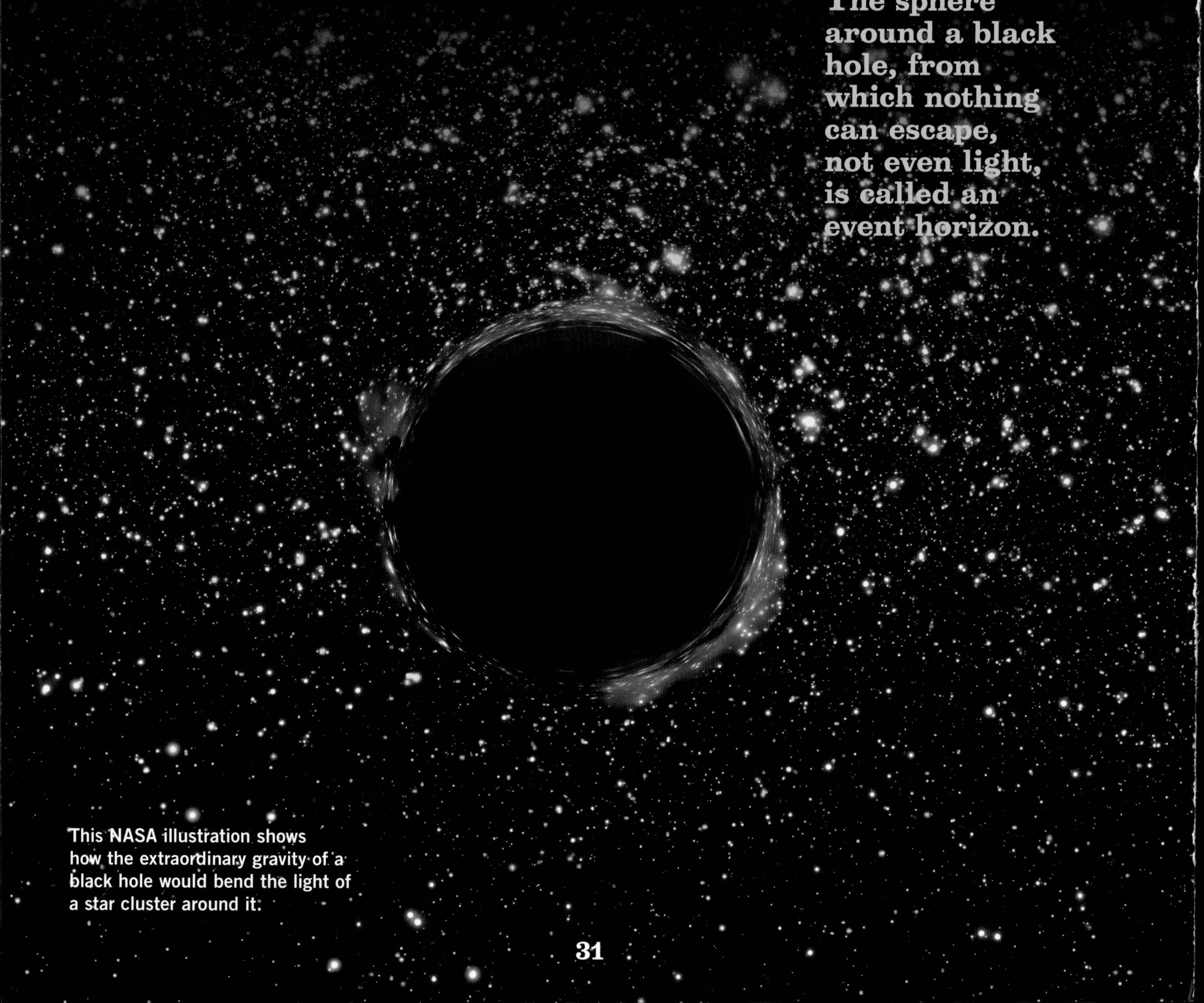

This NASA illustration shows how the extraordinary gravity of a black hole would bend the light of a star cluster around it.

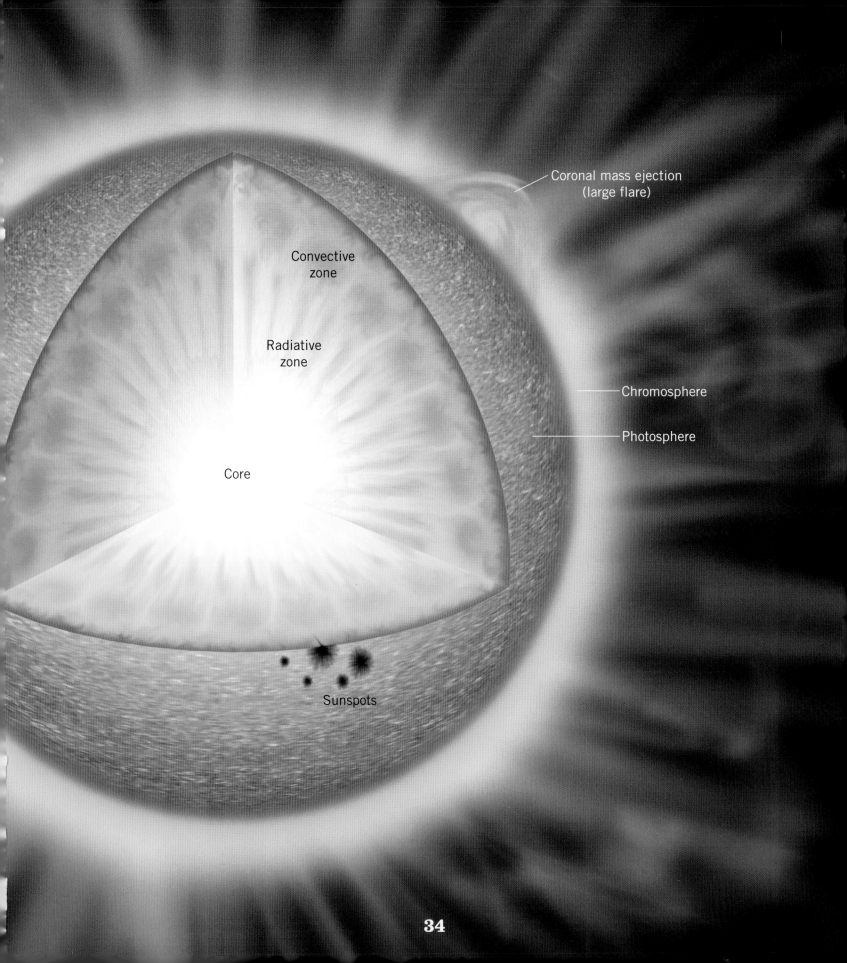

Coronal mass ejection
(large flare)

Convective
zone

Radiative
zone

Chromosphere

Photosphere

Core

Sunspots

Inside the Sun

Inside the Sun are three different regions. At the center is its core. The weight of the whole Sun creates enormous pressure here, resulting in temperatures higher than 27 million degrees F (15 million degrees C). That's hot enough for nuclear fusion to take place. The energy resulting from the nuclear fusion spreads out through the region just outside the core, which is called the radiative zone. This can take tens of thousands of years.

Outside the radiative zone lies a region where rising motions of the gas carry the energy the rest of the way out to the visible surface of the Sun in just a few months. This is the convective zone. The gas motions in this zone look a bit like the convection in water just before it boils.

Word Power

CORONA: the million-degree outermost layer of many stars, which is so hot that gas escapes the star's gravity and flows out into space as a stellar wind.

CONVECTION: the rising of heated material and falling of cooled material in a region heated from below and cooled from above, such as a pot of water about to boil or the interior of a star.

Solar wind

Solar flare

Corona

THE SUN

The Sun is like a power plant that makes life on our planet possible. Deep inside its core, nuclear fusion produces the light and heat we need to live. While we think of the Sun as special, it is actually just a regular, middle-aged star, a little more massive than the average star. It has been shining for about 4.6 billion years, and will remain stable for another 5 billion years or so.

Temperatur on the surfa of the Sun a roughly 10,0 (5,500°C).

This image in ultraviolet light shows the Sun's corona. Different colors indicate varying gas temperatures. Reds are relatively "cool" at around 10,000°C (18,000°F), while blues and greens are hotter—millions of degrees hotter!

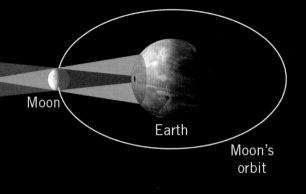

Sun

Moon

Earth

Moon's orbit

Solar Eclipse

During a solar eclipse, the Moon passes between the Sun and the Earth, and fully or partially covers the Sun as seen from the part of Earth in its shadow. At least two solar eclipses occur every year.

When the blazing photosphere is hidden by the Moon during an eclipse, the much fainter, but hotter, corona can be seen with the naked eye.

Sunspots come and go in cycles of 11 years.

How Scientists Study the Sun

Since it is impossible to get anywhere near a star like the Sun, you might be wondering how we know what goes on beneath its surface. Solar physicists use both ground-based and space-based telescopes to study the Sun.

In space, satellite telescopes have given us a detailed look at the Sun in ultraviolet and X-ray light, letting us see the Sun's energetic magnetic field and the heating of its corona. On the ground, a major advance has been the realization that the Sun rings like a bell, although with an extremely low tone of one vibration every few minutes, rather than hundreds of vibrations a second. Just as geologists learn about the inside of the Earth by measuring and studying earthquakes, solar physicists can measure the ringing of the Sun to learn about its inner structure.

Sunspots are dark regions on the Sun where its magnetic field is strongest. They are cooler regions, with temperatures of "only" 6,300°F (3,500°C), which is 3,600°F (2,000°C) cooler than the rest of the Sun's surface.

The Sun's Surface

The radiative and convective zones are so dense that light cannot pass through them. This density drops with distance from the center of the Sun, though, and when it drops low enough, the solar atmosphere becomes transparent to light. The energy that we see (light) and feel (heat) on Earth escapes from the visible surface of the Sun, which is called the photosphere.

Churning magnetic fields generated in the convective zone pass through the photosphere. The magnetic fields carry energy from the roiling gas motions in the convective zone out into the upper atmospheric layers of the Sun, called the chromosphere and corona. This heats the corona to temperatures of many millions of degrees. The corona is faintly visible during total eclipses of the Sun.

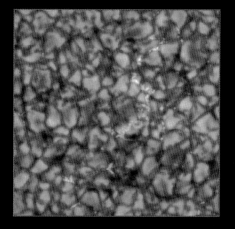

In this greatly magnified image of the Sun's surface, energy escaping from the center is producing convection. The lighter areas show where hotter gas is rising from below, while the darker areas reveal where cooler gas is sinking back down.

Word Power

MAGNETIC FIELD: the forces produced by moving, electrically charged material, such as the ionized gas in a star's convective zone.

A solar flare is a massive explosion on the Sun that happens when energy stored in the Sun's magnetic fields is suddenly released.

Prominences are huge clouds of relatively cool dense plasma exploding into the Sun's hot, thin corona.

35

SPACE WEATHER

Although we are almost 93 million miles (150 million kilometers) from the Sun, what happens that far away in space can affect us here on Earth. Storms on the Sun, such as solar flares, have the power to disrupt satellite broadcasts and global positioning systems, and to damage electrical power grids. Luckily, the Earth itself has a powerful magnetic field that protects us from the worst of space weather.

Use your smartphone to scan here and learn more about space weather.

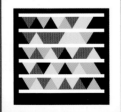

The Earth's Magnetosphere

The Earth's own magnetic field protects it from the charged particles of the solar wind and solar flares. The region within the Earth's magnetic field is called the magnetosphere. Although "sphere" is in its name, the magnetosphere is not actually a sphere around the Earth. Instead, the solar wind pushes it toward the Earth on the Sun-facing side, and causes a "tail" to form on the dark side of the planet.

THE SOLAR WIND

The outer atmosphere of the Sun is so hot that the Sun's gravity can't hold it down. Gas streams away from the Sun in all directions, at speeds reaching a million miles an hour (almost two million kilometers an hour). This solar wind carries the Sun's magnetic field along with it and sweeps across the entire solar system.

SOLAR FLARES

A solar flare (or stellar flare, if it happens on any other star) is an explosion on the Sun (or other star) that occurs when strong magnetic fields get tangled, which causes them to release their energy. The largest solar flares blow away huge amounts of hot gas from the corona. These storms, called coronal mass ejections, are the "hurricanes" of space weather. They are the largest and most dangerous.

The aurora borealis, or northern lights, are a result of charged particles from the solar wind becoming trapped by the Earth's magnetic field. They ionize—or give an electric charge to—the atmosphere when they hit it, causing it to glow.

MULTIPLE
STAR SYSTEMS

Imagine two stars bound together by gravity, flinging each other around like dance partners as they orbit each other. About half of all stars live out their lives like this. A system of two stars orbiting each other is called a binary star. If they have a third star orbiting them, it's called a triple system. A binary star can even orbit another binary pair, which is known as a quadruple system. Scientists have found that the more massive a star is, the more likely it is to be in a multiple star system.

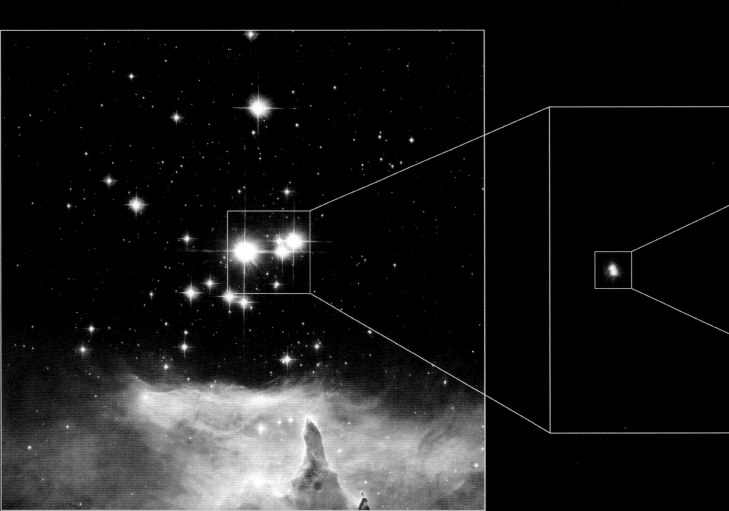

Seeing Binary Stars

Most binary stars orbit so closely to one another that even with a telescope they cannot be seen as separate objects. However, some do orbit far enough away from each other that we can observe them as two stars. Some stars on closer orbits are aligned so that one star passes in front of the other, eclipsing it when viewed from Earth. The star in front blocks light from the star behind, so that together they appear dimmer than when they are separated. Such systems are called eclipsing binaries. Many other kinds of binaries can be identified with careful measurements of the combined light from the two stars.

Once, the star Pismis 24-1 was thought to be a single star with an incredibly large mass 200 to 300 times larger than our Sun. But new observations have revealed that it is actually two separate stars orbiting each other.

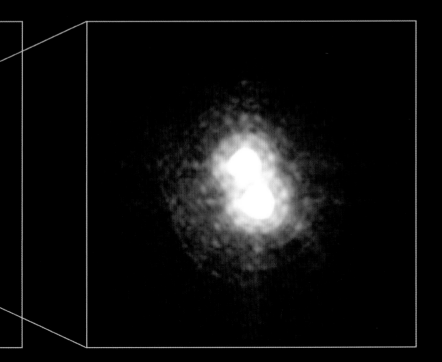

A massive, dense, white dwarf star steals gas from a lower-mass (yet larger) red companion star.

Stellar Cannibalism

Like all stars, those in a binary system change over their lifetimes. This can be dangerous to their partners if they orbit too closely. When the more massive star in a binary pair reaches the end of its life, it swells up, forming a red giant whose diameter is larger than the orbit of the Earth. The red giant can swallow whole any partner in an orbit that comes too close. Usually the two stars then merge into one massive star. However, if the partner is large enough, it can sometimes drive away the red giant's atmosphere instead. The partner is then left in orbit around the remaining tiny, but dense and massive, white dwarf core. That orbit would have been inside the original

THE STARS AND YOU

We've learned a lot about stars over the last few centuries. Thanks to great improvements in technology that allow astronomers to see farther and farther into space, new discoveries are being made all the time. But there is still a lot to learn. We still don't know, for example, what determines the masses of newly forming stars, or how red giants lose their outer layers. Continuing to study the Universe will bring us closer to solving these mysteries.

Look Up!

Nonprofessional astronomers have been responsible over the years for discoveries that help us learn more about the stars. With just a basic telescope, an Internet connection, and a lot of enthusiasm, you, too, may be able to add to our knowledge about the stars. For example, thousands of people have helped classify galaxies from a survey by the Hubble Space Telescope at www.galaxyzoo.org, and many others watch variable stars (stars that change in brightness) for unusual behavior with backyard telescopes, reporting their findings to the American Association of Variable Star Observers.

STARS ACTIVITY
Stargazing

The night sky is like a giant puzzle. Hidden among the thousands of stars you can find dozens of constellations. You can also search for individual stars and planets. With a good star map, there's no limit to what you can find.

What You'll Need

- notebook
- pencil
- flashlight
- compass
- star map (Magazines such as *Natural History* and *Sky & Telescope* publish maps and listings of what you can expect to find in the night sky. Or download a star map from www.skyandtelescope. com/howto/basics/3308331.html)

Record Your Observations

Making a drawing of the sky can be tricky at first. Here are some tips:

1. Use a pencil. This will make it easier to move a star!

2. Draw a circle that's at least 5 inches (13 centimeters) across in your journal. This will represent the horizon on all sides.

3. Figure out which way is North using your compass. Mark it on the edge of the circle.

4. Draw in some landmarks you see at the horizon, such as trees and buildings. This will help you keep track of which way you're looking. It will also help you compare observations from different days.

5. Look straight up. Record what you see in the middle of the circle. Use little circles or dots to show the stars.

6. Make a note of the date, time, and who made the observations with you. Later, this information will help you identify what you saw.

7. Note the weather conditions, the place, and any notes about what the sky looked like.

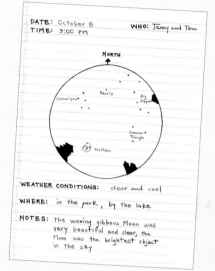

Do's & Don'ts

Do's:

- Let someone know you're going out at night. Or better yet, bring someone along to help search the sky.
- Bring a flashlight with a red filter to help you find your way and to see your notebook, compass, or sky map. If you don't have a red filter, wrap a piece of red plastic wrap or paper around the end of your flashlight.
- Get away from any distracting house lights or floodlights.
- Give your eyes a half hour to adjust to the darkness.
- Bring binoculars or a telescope to get a better look.

Don'ts:

- Don't ever go out at night without your parents' permission.
- Don't wander around. It's easy to get lost, so keep track of where you are. Remember to hold your notebook so your mark for North always points North.

Stars in the Big Dipper

#	Star Name	Distance from Earth in Light-Years	String Length
1	Alkaid	210	7 5/16 inches (18 1/2 centimeters)
2	Mizar	88	10 13/16 inches (27 1/2 centimeters)
3	Alioth	631	0 inches
4	Megrez	631	0 inches
5	Phecda	90	10 3/4 inches (27 1/3 centimeters)
6	Merak	88	11 inches (28 centimeters)
7	Dubhe	105	10 1/2 inches (26 2/3 centimeters)

Build the Big Dipper

When you look up into the night sky, the Big Dipper looks like a connect-the-dots picture on a piece of paper. But if you flew out in a spaceship and looked at the same stars from the side, it wouldn't look like a dipper anymore. The stars are actually nowhere near each other.

To find out what you'd see, build the Big Dipper!

What You'll Need

- a black crayon or marker
- an 8½ x 11–inch (21½ x 28–centimeter) piece of rigid cardboard or foam board
- seven black strings or threads, each about 2 feet (61 centimeters) long
- aluminum foil, cut into seven 6-inch (15-centimeter) squares
- pen or pencil to poke a hole in the cardboard
- tape
- ruler
- Big Dipper Map (download it from amnh.org/ology/features/stufftodo_astro/The_Big_Dipper.pdf)

What to Do

1. Print the Big Dipper Map. Color in the background to look like space. Glue or tape the map to the cardboard or foam board.

2. Poke holes through the cardboard where the seven "stars" appear on the paper.

3. Tape the end of a string to a square of foil. Crumple the foil into a ball around the string. Make the foil ball as tight as you can. Repeat this six times until you have seven foil ball stars on strings.

4. Poke the free end of a string through the hole for Star #1, Alkaid. On the chart, you'll see that Alkaid gets a string 7 5/16 inches (18½ centimeters) long. Pull the thread through the hole until the foil ball hangs 7 5/16 inches (18½ centimeters) from the board. Tape the thread in place on the backside of the board.

5. Repeat for all seven threads. Be careful not to let the strings get tangled together as you work. For stars #3 and #4, pull the string up until the ball hits the board and tape the string down in back.

6. You've done it! Tape your Big Dipper model to the ceiling or ask someone to hold it above you. Now stand or lie under it and look up. What do you see? This is like the view from Earth.

7. Now look at your mobile from different angles. That's what the Big Dipper looks like from space— and you didn't have to spend centuries traveling on a spaceship to see it!

Visit the Museum

The American Museum of Natural History is located in the heart of New York City. One of the world's most respected scientific and cultural institutions, the Museum is renowned for its exhibitions and collections, which serve as a field guide to the entire planet and present a panorama of the world's cultures. Visit the Museum's Rose Center for Earth and Space, which includes the Hayden Planetarium, to learn more about stars and the nature of the universe.

OLogy

The website of the American Museum of Natural History has a special place just for kids. Go to www.amnh.org/ology to do activities, play games, and explore more about stars.

Words to Know

Asteroids objects smaller than dwarf planets that are not round, but still orbit stars, and shine by reflected light.

Astronomer or Astrophysicist scientist who studies the Universe and its contents, including stars and galaxies.

Dark matter an invisible substance that makes up around 87 percent of the mass of the Universe. It has only been detected by its gravitational influence on its surroundings.

Density the amount of mass in a given volume. For example, a piece of lead is much heavier (has more mass) than a piece of foam of the same size, because lead is denser than foam.

Dwarf planets planets that are similar in size to other objects in their orbit around their parent star.

Element a substance containing only atoms that all have the same number of protons.

Gamma ray the form of light with the shortest wavelength.

Gravity the force of attraction between any two objects.

Light energy energy carried in the form of waves through electric and magnetic fields. Types of light include radio, infrared, visible, ultraviolet, X-ray, and gamma ray.

Mass the amount of material that makes up an object. Mass determines how much objects weigh when gravity pulls on them, and how hard they are to move.

Neutron star the final state of many massive stars after they explode as a supernova at the end of their lives (some massive stars become black holes instead). It is extremely dense and about the size of a city.

Optical telescope measures visible light given off (emitted) or reflected by stars and other distant objects.

Photosphere the layer of a star where it becomes transparent, and where light escapes into space.

Radiation energy that travels in the form of rays or waves (waves such as light, radio, X-rays, and gamma rays), or in the form of subatomic particles.

Radiative zone the layer of a star through which energy slowly filters in the form of radiation.

Radio telescope measures radio waves from stars and other distant objects.

Solar flare a magnetic explosion on the Sun that produces storms in the solar wind and generates dangerous radiation.

Star cluster a group of many stars orbiting each other tightly.

Stellar core the center of a star, where nuclear fusion generates intense energy.

Sunspots darker, cooler areas on the Sun's photosphere that form where the magnetic field is strongest.

Bibliography

Freedman, Roger, A. *Universe: Stars and Galaxies*. W.H. Freeman & Company: New York, 2010.

Grego, Peter. *The Universe*. Collins: London, 2006.

Lamber, David. *The Kingfisher Book of the Universe*. Kingfisher: New York, 2001.

Lang, Kenneth R. *The Cambridge Encyclopedia of the Sun*. Cambridge University Press: Cambridge, 2001.

Rees, Martin. *Universe: The Definitive Visual Guide*. Dorling Kindersly: London, 2005.

Tyson, Neil deGrasse, Charles Liu, and Robert Irion. *One Universe: At Home in the Cosmos*. Joseph Henry Press: Washington, DC, 2000.

Find Out More

Books to Read

Couper, Heather and Nigel Henbest. *Encyclopedia of Space*. Dorling Kindersley: New York, 2009.

Dickinson, Terence. *NightWatch: A Practical Guide to Viewing the Universe*. Firefly Books: Ontario, 2006.

Dyer, Alan. *Space*. Simon & Schuster Children's Publishing: New York, 2007.

Kerrod, Robin. *Universe*. Dorling Kindersley Eyewitness Books: New York, 2009.

Lippincott, Kristen. *Astronomy*. Dorling Kindersley Eyewitness Books: New York, 2008.

Moche, Dinah, L. *Astronomy: A Self-Teaching Guide*. John Wiley and Sons: Hoboken, 2009.

Rey, H. A. *Find the Constellations* (revised edition). Houghton Mifflin Harcourt: Boston, 2008.

Websites to Visit

American Association of Variable Star Observers
www.aavso.org

American Museum of Natural History
www.amnh.org
www.amnh.org/rose
www.amnh.org/rose/spaceshow/journey
www.amnh.org/ology
www.amnh.org/ology/astronomy

Page 11 smartphone link:
www.amnh.org/insidebooks/starsprelude

Page 20 smartphone link:
www.amnh.org/insidebooks/starpics

Page 38 smartphone link:
www.amnh.org/insidebooks/spaceweather

NASA Kids' Club
http://kids.msfc.nasa.gov

Sky & Telescope Magazine
www.skyandtelescope.com/howto/basics

Index